PUERTO RICO

A TRUE BOOK

by

Elaine Landau

Children's Press®
A Division of Grolier Publishing
New York London Hong Kong Sydney
Danbury, Connecticut

A young lace maker

Reading Consultant
Linda Cornwell
*Coordinator of School Quality
and Professional Improvement
Indiana State Teachers
Association*

Author's Dedication
For Jessica Garmizo

Visit Children's Press® on the
Internet at:
http://publishing.grolier.com

Library of Congress Cataloging-in-Publication Data

Landau, Elaine.
Puerto Rico / by Elaine Landau.
      p.   cm. — (A True book)
   Includes bibliographical references and index.
   Summary: Discusses the geography, history, government, people, and
economy of the island nation of Puerto Rico.
   ISBN: 0-516-20986-8 (lib. bdg.)   0-516-26770-1 (pbk.)
   1. Puerto Rico—Juvenile literature. [1. Puerto Rico.] I. Title. II. Series.
F1958.3L36   1999
972.95—dc21
                                                                98-45092
                                                                CIP
                                                                AC

GROLIER
PUBLISHING

Contents

The El Yunque mountains (left) and brightly colored flowers (below), are two of the many spectacular features found in Puerto Rico.

Island of Enchantment

Close your eyes and picture a beautiful island with sandy beaches and brightly colored flowers. Delicious fruits and nuts hang from the trees, and tiny tree frogs hop around. A string of mountains stretches from east to west across this island. And a magnificent rain forest stands on the slope of a mountain. If you think this is an imaginary paradise, you're wrong. You've been reading about Puerto Rico.

Puerto Rico is an island in the West Indies. The small nearby islands of Culebra, Mona, and Vieques, are considered part of Puerto Rico. Including these islands, Puerto Rico covers an area of 3,427 square miles (8,876 square kilometers).

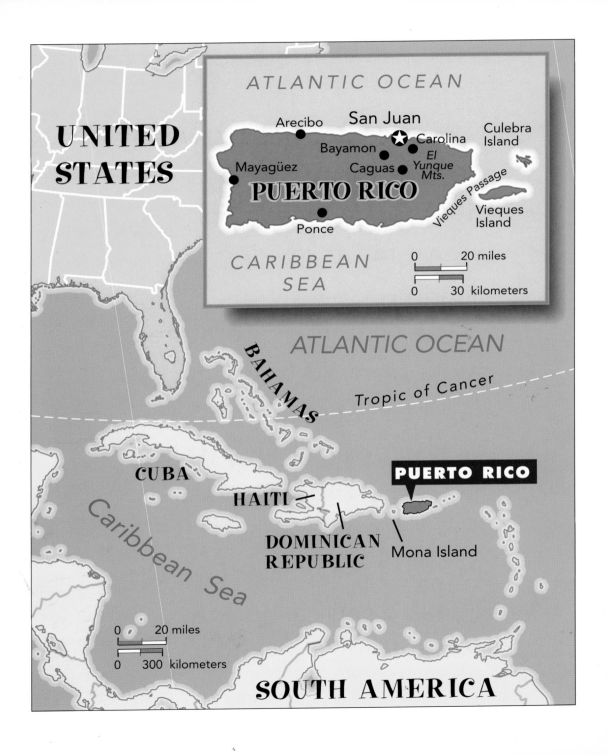

Puerto Rico lies between the Caribbean Sea and the Atlantic Ocean and is known for its inviting climate.

The winter temperatures range from 70 to 75 degrees Fahrenheit (21 to 24 degrees Celsius), while summer temperatures are about 80° Fahrenheit (27° C). No wonder Puerto Rico is often called the Island of Enchantment.

Commonwealth of Puerto Rico

Puerto Rico is a commonwealth of the United States. As a commonwealth, its more than 3 million people enjoy many of the same benefits as people do in the United States. Puerto Ricans are U.S. citizens and can travel to or live in the United States at any time.

Most federal laws that affect the states apply to Puerto Rico as well. An elected commissioner from Puerto Rico represents the island's interests in Congress.

However, elected officials in Puerto Rico pass laws that affect the island. As a commonwealth, Puerto Rico has its own constitution, Senate, and House of Representatives. Its chief executive officer (or head of government) is a governor.

Citizens of
Puerto Rico

History

Christopher Columbus arrived in Puerto Rico November 19, 1493. He was on his second voyage to the New World when he first saw this beautiful island. At that time, 50,000 to 70,000 Indians lived there, but they could not defend themselves against the well-

Columbus called Puerto Rico *San Juan Bautista*, meaning Saint John the Baptist.

armed Spaniards who settled there in the years that followed. Many Indians were killed in unsuccessful revolts against the invaders. Others were enslaved by the Spanish and died from the brutal treatment. Many other Indians died from diseases brought by the Europeans.

After most of the Indians on the island had died, the Spanish brought in another source of free labor. In 1518, the first African slaves arrived. Some worked the Spaniards' sugarcane, tobacco, cotton, ginger, and indigo crops. Others labored in the island's

This painting depicts slaves working on a cotton plantation.

gold mines. In 1873, slavery was peacefully banned in Puerto Rico.

Other European countries soon realized how desirable Puerto Rico was. Both the English and the Dutch tried

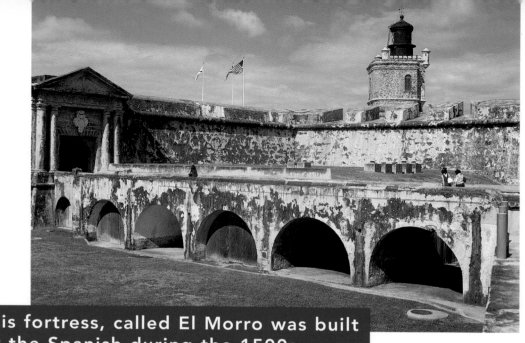

This fortress, called El Morro was built by the Spanish during the 1500s.

to take over the island, but these attempts failed. The English captured San Juan in 1598, but left after several weeks. The Spanish population grew gradually. They built fortresses and kept their settlements well armed.

Puerto Rico remained a Spanish colony until the Spanish-American War in 1898. The Americans won the war against Spain, and Puerto Rico was given to the United States under the terms of the 1898 peace treaty.

Life in Puerto Rico began to get better. Over time, United States corporations invested in the island, and more schools and hospitals were built. In the 1940s, with U.S. cooperation,

Puerto Rican leaders started a program known as Operation Bootstrap. The project's goal was to further enhance the lives of Puerto Ricans. During this period, thousands of Puerto Ricans migrated to the United States.

Through Operation Boot-strap, slums in Puerto Rico were cleared away, and new housing was built. Farm areas were fairly divided among peo-ple who worked on the land,

Under Operation Bootstrap, these new homes were built.

and more money went to the island's educational system. In the years following Operation Bootstrap, various economic projects were developed to help boost the industry.

In September 1998, Hurricane Georges hit Puerto Rico. More than $400 million was given to victims, making it the most costly hurricane in U.S. history.

Although these programs were helpful, Puerto Rico has many other problems. The unemployment rate is still high, forcing many Puerto Ricans to live in poverty. The island also had to deal with many natural disasters, such as mud slides and hurricanes.

Some Puerto Ricans would like their island to become a U.S. state. Others want it to be an independent country. But in an election on December 13, 1998, the majority of Puerto Ricans voted to have their island remain a U.S. commonwealth. It was the third time since 1969 that the Puerto Rican people had voted this way.

The People

While most Puerto Ricans are of Spanish descent, people of other nationalities live there too. Some Puerto Ricans are descendants of the island's first Indian people's. Other families are related to the African slaves that were brought to Puerto Rico many years ago.

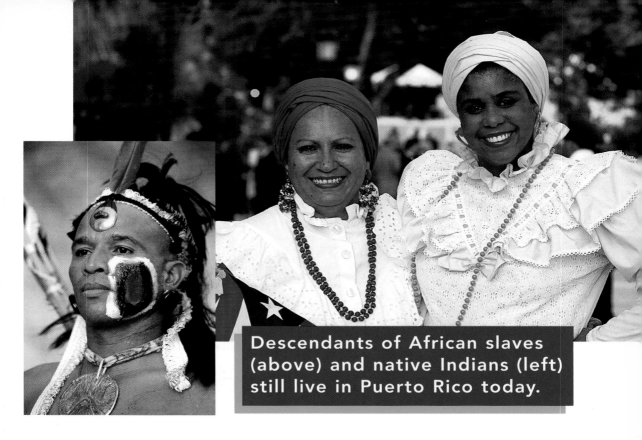

Descendants of African slaves (above) and native Indians (left) still live in Puerto Rico today.

The majority of Puerto Ricans are Roman Catholics, although other religions are practiced on the island.

At one time, there were two classes of people on the

island—a small wealthy upper class, and a large number of poor people. This was mainly because so many people could not find jobs. Recently, however, more people have found good jobs, and a middle class has developed in Puerto Rico. Government programs have also helped improve living conditions for people with lower incomes.

About 3.8 million people live in Puerto Rico today, and parts of the island are quite

San Juan is a unique city where one can escape a noisy, crowded street (left) for a peaceful day at the beach (below).

crowded. Before the 1960s, more than half of Puerto Rico's population lived in rural, countryside regions. Today, about two-thirds of the people live in cities. Puerto Rico's capital city of San Juan and its surrounding area are among the most heavily populated. More than 400,000 people live in San Juan.

Although Puerto Rico has a strong Spanish flavor, it is similar in many ways to the United States. Both Spanish and English are the island's official languages, and English is taught in the schools. Puerto Rico's public school system was established by the

U.S. government. As a result, its many schools are much like schools in the United States. The island also has shopping plazas, housing developments, and highways.

A shopping mall in Ponce

FOX DELICIAS MALL

Most Puerto Ricans enjoy sporting activities. The island's favorite sport is baseball. Many outstanding baseball players from Puerto Rico have played for major league baseball teams in the United States.

Basketball, weight lifting, boxing, and swimming are also popular. Of course, deep-sea diving is a special treat in Puerto Rico, with its underwater world of colorful coral and unusual tropical fish.

Roberto Clemente

Roberto Clemente, the Puerto Rican Hall of Famer, was one of the world's greatest baseball players. Born in Carolina, Puerto Rico, in 1934, Clemente played for the Pittsburgh Pirates. He helped lead the Pirates to victory in the World Series in both 1960 and 1971. Clemente was named outstanding player of the 1971 World Series, and also won four National League batting titles.

Clemente died in a plane crash in 1971. He was on his way to aid earthquake victims in Nicaragua.

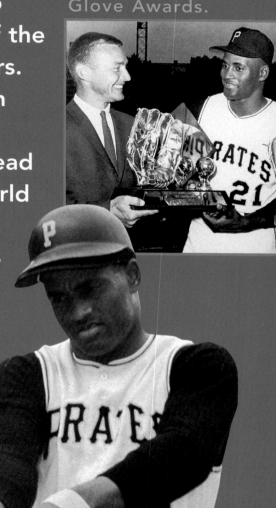

Clemente received twelve career Gold Glove Awards.

The Economy

Farming is important to Puerto Rico's economy. More than half of its land is farmland. For many years, the island's chief crops included coffee, sugar-cane, and tobacco. Vegetables and fruits, such as bananas, coconuts, and oranges, have long been grown on the

A farm worker tends to a banana crop.

island. In recent times, however, the number of dairy
and poultry farms, has
increased. These provide a
much-needed source of milk,
eggs, chicken, and beef for
the islanders.

Today, manufacturing is a
major source of income in
Puerto Rico. Its factories pro-
duce clothing, scientific and
electrical instruments, rum,
processed foods, paper, fur-
niture, plastics, prescription

drugs, leather goods, and
various types of machinery.

Tourism in Puerto Rico is
also important. Each year, visitors from various countries
vacation on the island. Many

Snorkling is a favorite among tourists.

come to enjoy the beautiful beaches, the restaurants, and the nightlife. Others come to experience the special beauty and wonder of the tropical rain forest on El Yunque mountain.

Art and Culture

Reminders of Puerto Rico's history and culture are found throughout the island. The old churches and fortresses are fine examples of classic Spanish architecture. Puerto Rico's many holiday celebrations feature traditional island dance, music, and costumes.

Plena is among Puerto Rico's best-known types of music. Set against African rhythms, the songs tell about life in Puerto Rico. Another popular form of music is salsa, known for its lively, vigorous beat. Salsa blends Latin rhythms with elements of jazz, rock, and soul music.

In addition, Puerto Rico has a rich writing heritage. Through the years, its authors have often written about social and political issues. The jíbaro, a folklore figure representing a farmworker, is a popular character in Puerto Rican literature.

Old San Juan is a colorful part of Puerto Rico's capital city, with its museums, landmarks, and unusual shops.

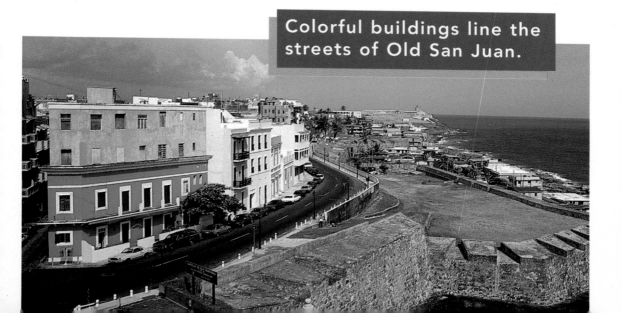

Colorful buildings line the streets of Old San Juan.

Colonial houses and other buildings have been restored to their original state.

Ponce, Puerto Rico's second-oldest city, is another cultural center. It is home to numerous art galleries, theaters, museums, professional schools, and universities. The Ponce Museum of Art has the finest art collection in the Caribbean.

One especially interesting structure in Ponce is its

Ponce is known for its
well-preserved neighborhoods.

Indian Heritage

Puerto Rico's Indian heritage is celebrated at Tibes Indian Ceremonial Park just outside of Ponce. It is one of the oldest-known burial grounds in the Caribbean. Indian plazas dating from A.D. 700 and 1,800-year-old skeletons have been unearthed there. The park also includes ceremonial ball courts, dance grounds, and exhibits of Indian pottery and jewelry.

Tibes Indian huts

An Indian burial ground

unusual museum firehouse— the Parque de Bombas. The firehouse, painted bright red with black stripes, was built in 1883. Antique firetrucks and other reminders of the past are on display here.

The Parque de Bombas

While Old San Juan and Ponce have drawn countless visitors over the years, Puerto Rico's art and culture are also enjoyed by the local people. The island's Department of Parks and Recreation sponsors plays, music, and folk-dancing classes. A number of book-mobiles and traveling exhibits also tour the island.

Puerto Rico means "rich port" in Spanish. And, in

The Cathedral of Our Lady of Guadalupe in Ponce

countless ways, this island is rich in beauty, culture, and charm.

To Find Out More

Here are some additional resources to help you learn more about Puerto Rico:

 **Books**

Mayor, T. W. **The Caribbean and Its People.** Thompson Learning, 1995.

McKinley, Yvonne. **A Taste of the Caribbean.** Thompson Learning, 1995.

Petersen, David. **North America.** Children's Press, 1998.

Thompson, Kathleen. **Puerto Rico.** Raintree Steck-Vaughn, 1996.

West, Alan. **Roberto Clemente: Baseball Legend.** Millbrook Press, 1993.

Organizations and Online Sites

The Official Roberto Clemente Website
http://www. robertoclemente21.com

Dedicated and maintained by the Clemente family, this site provides an in-depth look at the life and accomplishments of this legendary baseball player.

Sports:Puerto Rico
http:users.aol.com/boriken 01/sports.htm

From baseball to peewee football, this site provides links to Puerto Rico's favorite sports.

Welcome to Puerto Rico
http://welcome. topuertorico.org/

A wide range of information about the island of Puerto Rico can be found at this site, including its history, culture, and the people.

World Wide Travel Source:Puerto Rico
http://www. wwtravelsource.com/ puertorico.htm

This site provides links to the best travel spots in Puerto Rico. From national parks to underwater sea travel, this site has it all.

Important Words

architecture the art of designing and building structures

indigo a plant from which a dark blue dye can be made

landmark an important or historic place

majority more than half of a given group

poultry farmbirds raised for their eggs and meat

rural having to do with the country-side

treaty an agreement between nations

Index

Meet the Author

Popular author Elaine Landau worked as a newspaper reporter, editor, and a youth services librarian before becoming a full-time writer. She has written more than one hundred non-fiction books for young people, including many books for Franklin Watts and Children's Press. Ms. Landau, who has a bachelor's degree in English and journalism from New York University and a master's degree in library and information science from Pratt Institute, lives in Miami, Florida, with her husband and son.

Photographs ©: Archive Photos: 29 top (Sporting News); Corbis-Bettmann: 19, 29 bottom (UPI); D. Donne Bryant Stock Photography: 15 (D. Donne Bryant), 4 top, 23 right (Suzanne Murphy-Larronde); Gamma-Liaison, Inc.: 20 (Andre Kang); Michael Defreitas: (Elizabeth Holmes), 39 (Tony Perrottet); Photo Researchers: 13 (Jean-Loup Charmet/SPL), 33 (Tom Hollyman), cover (F. Stuart Westmorland); Robert Fried Photography: 25 bottom; Superstock, Inc.: 40 top (Max & Bea Hunn), 16; Suzanne Murphy-Larronde: 1, 2, 4 bottom, 11, 23 left, 41; The Image Works: 27 (Macduff Everton), 25 top (Sven Martson), 31 (K. McGlynn); Tony Stone Images: 43 (Stuart Westmorland).
Map by Joe LeMonnier